science for a changing world

Hurricane Gustav: Observations and Analysis of Coastal Change

By Kara S. Doran, Hilary F. Stockdon, Nathaniel G. Plant, Asbury H. Sallenger, Kristy K. Guy, and Katherine A. Serafin

Open-File Report 2009–1279

U.S. Department of the Interior
U.S. Geological Survey

U.S. Department of the Interior
KEN SALAZAR, Secretary

U.S. Geological Survey
Suzette M. Kimball, Acting Director

U.S. Geological Survey, Reston, Virginia 2009

For product and ordering information:
World Wide Web: http://www.usgs.gov/pubprod
Telephone: 1-888-ASK-USGS

For more information on the USGS—the Federal source for science about the Earth,
its natural and living resources, natural hazards, and the environment:
World Wide Web: http://www.usgs.gov
Telephone: 1-888-ASK-USGS

Suggested citation:

Doran, K.S., Stockdon, H.F., Plant, N.G., Sallenger, A.H., Guy, K.K., and Serafin, K.A., 2009, Hurricane Gustav:
Observations of coastal change: U.S. Geological Survey Open-File Report 2009-1279, 35 p.

Contents

Figures

iv

Tables

Conversion Factors

SI to Inch/Pound

Multiply	By	To obtain
Length		
centimeter (cm)	0.3937	inch (in.)
millimeter (mm)	0.03937	inch (in.)
meter (m)	3.281	foot (ft)
kilometer (km)	0.6214	mile (mi)
kilometer (km)	0.5400	mile, nautical (nmi)
meter (m)	1.094	yard (yd)
Area		
square meter (m^2)	0.0002471	acre
square kilometer (km^2)	247.1	acre
square meter (m^2)	10.76	square foot (ft^2)
square kilometer (km^2)	0.3861	square mile (mi^2)
Volume		
cubic meter (m^3)	35.31	cubic foot (ft^3)
cubic meter (m^3)	1.308	cubic yard (yd^3)
Flow rate		
kilometer per hour (km/h)	0.6214	mile per hour (mi/h)

Vertical coordinate information is referenced to North American Vertical Datum of 1988 (NAVD 88)
Horizontal coordinate information is referenced to the North American Datum of 1983 (NAD 83)

Additional Abbreviations and Acronyms

ACRONYM OR ABBREVIATION	DEFINITION
CORS	Continuously Operating Reference Stations
DEM	Digital Elevation Model
EAARL	Experimental Advanced Airborne Research Lidar
GPS	Global Positioning System
Hz	Hertz

kHz	Kilohertz
KHSA	Stennis Airport
Lidar	Light Detection and Ranging
NAD83	North American Datum 1983
NAVD88	North American Vertical Datum 1988
NHC	National Hurricane Center
nm	Nanometer(s)
NOAA	National Oceanic and Atmospheric Administration
NWC	National Weather Center
USGS	U.S. Geological Survey
UTC	Coordinated Universal Time

Hurricane Gustav: Observations and Analysis of Coastal Change

By Kara S. Doran, Hilary F. Stockdon, Nathaniel G. Plant, Asbury H. Sallenger, Kristy K. Guy, and Katherine A. Serafin

1. Introduction

Understanding storm-induced coastal change and forecasting these changes require knowledge of the physical processes associated with a storm and the geomorphology of the impacted coastline. The primary physical processes of interest are the wind field, storm surge, currents, and wave field. Not only does wind cause direct damage to structures along the coast, but it is ultimately responsible for much of the energy that is transferred to the ocean and expressed as storm surge, mean currents, and surface waves. Waves and currents are the processes most responsible for moving sediments in the coastal zone during extreme storm events. Storm surge, which is the rise in water level due to the wind, barometric pressure, and other factors, allows both waves and currents to attack parts of the coast not normally exposed to these processes.

Coastal geomorphology, including shapes of the shoreline, beaches, and dunes, is also a significant aspect of the coastal change observed during extreme storms. Relevant geomorphic variables include sand dune elevation, beach width, shoreline position, sediment grain size, and foreshore beach slope. These variables, in addition to hydrodynamic processes, can be used to predict coastal vulnerability to storms.

The U.S. Geological Survey (USGS) National Assessment of Coastal Change Hazards project (*http://coastal.er.usgs.gov/hurricanes*) strives to provide hazard information to those concerned about the Nation's coastlines, including residents of coastal areas, government agencies responsible for coastal management, and coastal researchers. As part of the National Assessment, observations were collected to measure morphological changes associated with Hurricane Gustav, which made landfall near Cocodrie, Louisiana, on September 1, 2008. Methods of observation included oblique aerial photography, airborne topographic surveys, and ground-based topographic surveys. This report documents these data-collection efforts and presents qualitative and quantitative descriptions of hurricane-induced changes to the shoreline, beaches, dunes, and infrastructure in the region that was heavily impacted by Hurricane Gustav.

The remainder of this report is divided into the following sections:

- Section 2, Storm Overview - presents a synopsis of the storm, including meteorological evolution, wind speed impact area, wind-wave generation, and storm-surge extent and magnitudes.
- Section 3, Coastal-Change Observations - describes data collection missions, including acquisition of oblique aerial photography and airborne light detection and ranging (lidar) topographic surveys, and observations of coastal change in response to Hurricane Gustav.
- Section 4, Coastal-Change Analysis - describes data-analysis methods and results.

2. Storm Overview

2.1 Storm History

Hurricane Gustav was an active tropical weather system in the Caribbean Sea and Gulf of Mexico from August 25 to September 2, 2008 (fig. 1; Beven and Kimberlain, 2009). On August 25 at 1500 Universal Time Coordinated (UTC), an area of disturbed weather in the Caribbean Sea, 415 kilometers (km) southeast of Haiti, was identified as a tropical depression. At 2000 UTC the same day, Tropical Storm Gustav became the seventh named storm of the 2008 hurricane season. Gustav strengthened to hurricane status on August 26 at 0820 UTC and made landfall in Haiti as a Category 1 hurricane the same day. Subsequent landfalls occurred near Kingston, Jamaica, on August 28, and the Cayman Islands, Isle of Youth, Cuba, and Pinar del Rio, Cuba, on August 30 before the storm entered the Gulf of Mexico on August 31 as a Category 3 hurricane. Hurricane Gustav made landfall near Cocodrie, Louisiana, as a strong Category 2 storm with maximum sustained winds of 170 kilometers per hour (km/h) on September 1, 2008, at 1500 UTC (Beven and Kimberlain, 2009).

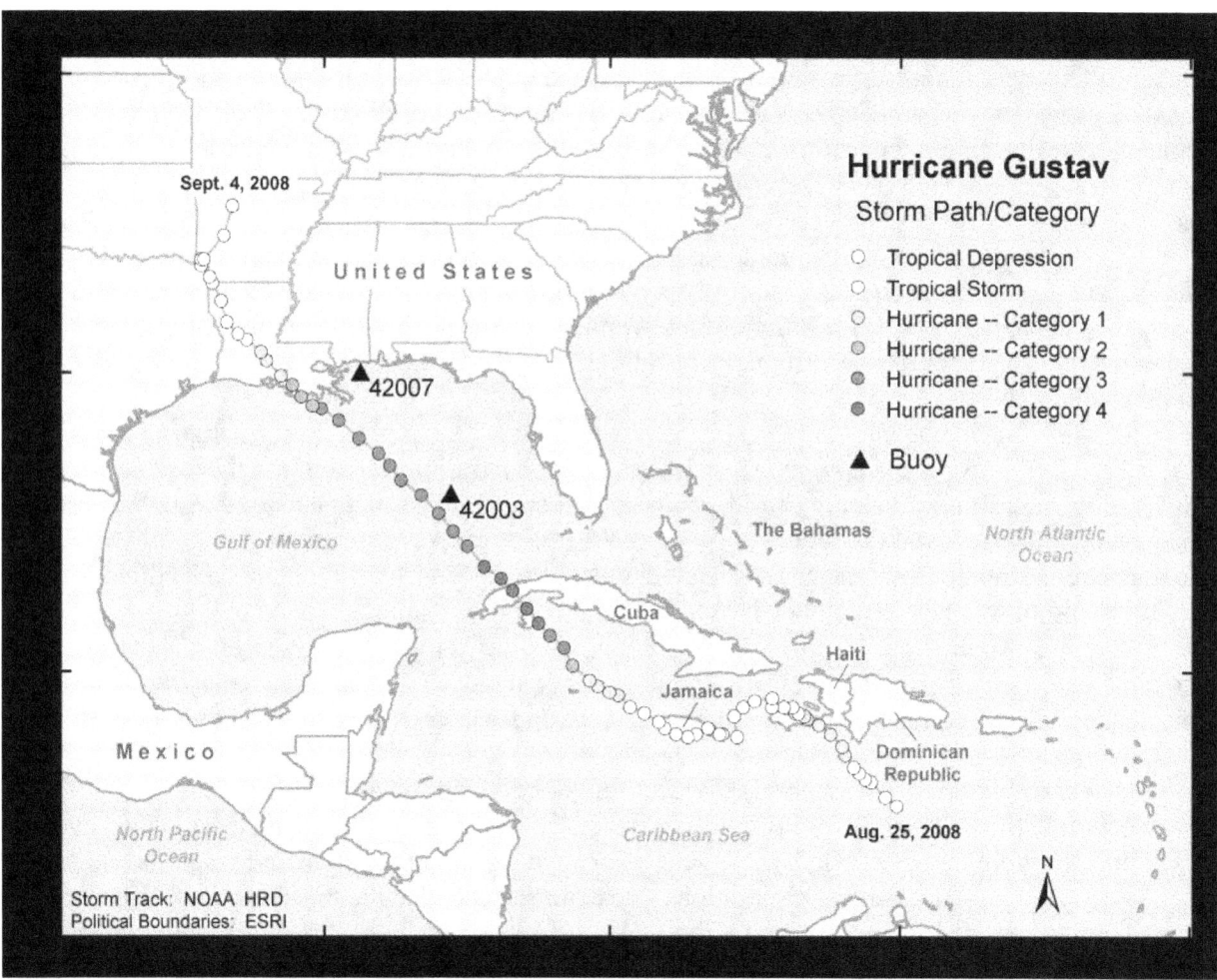

Figure 1. Track of Hurricane Gustav in the Caribbean Sea and Gulf of Mexico.

2.2 Extent of Hurricane-Force Winds

Maximum sustained winds estimated by the National Oceanic and Atmospheric Administration (NOAA) Atlantic Oceanographic and Meteorological Laboratory Hurricane Research Division (using methods described by Powell and others, 1998) indicate that hurricane-force winds impacted approximately 270 km of Louisiana's coastline. Wind speeds in excess of 119 km/h (hurricane force) extended from Marsh Island, across the central Louisiana barrier islands, to the eastern edge of the modern lobe of the Mississippi River delta (fig. 2). Maximum wind-speeds of 166 km/h were observed just east of Grand Isle, Louisiana.

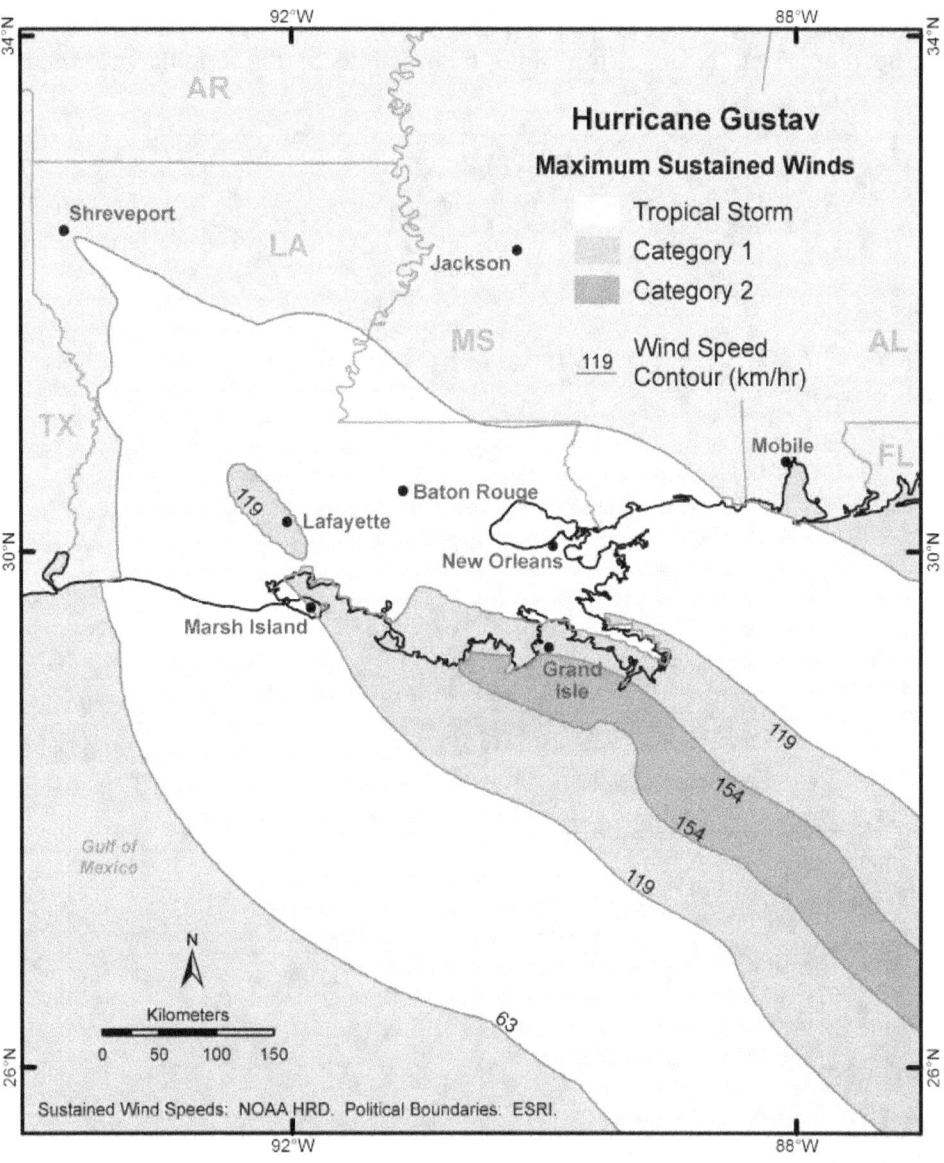

Figure 2. Wind speeds, in kilometers per hour (km/h), generated by Hurricane Gustav, as calculated by the National Oceanic and Atmospheric Administration Hurricane Research Division. The extent of hurricane-force wind, as defined by a category 1 wind speed of 119 km/h, is indicated by the light red contour.

2.3 Offshore Wave Climate

Several moored buoys operated by the NOAA National Data Buoy Center measured heights and periods of waves generated by Hurricane Gustav. Approximately 22 hours prior to landfall, Hurricane Gustav passed within 61 km of Buoy 42003 (fig. 1), which is located in the Gulf of Mexico, approximately 485 km south of Panama City, Florida. The maximum significant wave height recorded at this station was 10.5 meters (m) (National Data Buoy Center, 2008). Located closer to the coast, Buoy 42007 (fig. 1) recorded a maximum significant wave height of 6.6 m at 1000 UTC on September 1 (fig. 3), 5 hours before landfall (National Data Buoy Center, 2008). This station, positioned in 14 m water depth, was located outside of the extent of hurricane force winds, approximately 190 km to the east of the hurricane track near Biloxi, Mississippi. These waves were affected, and heights likely lowered, by dissipation as the waves propagated across the broad continental shelf. Some of the waves may also have been breaking, further diminishing their heights by the time they reached the 14-m depth station.

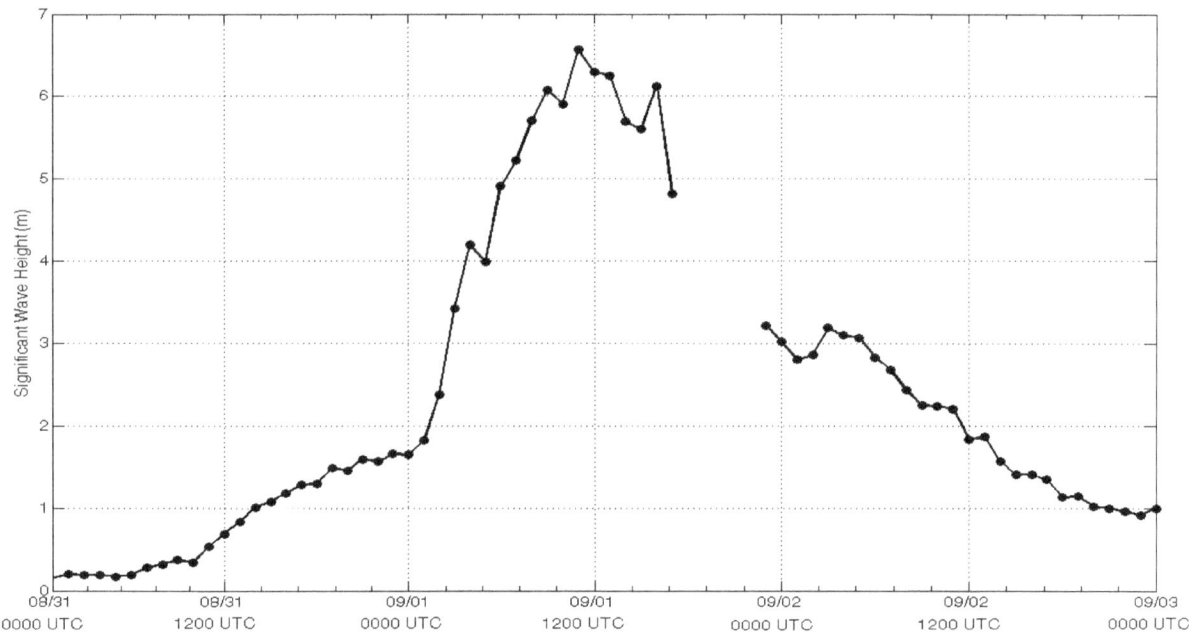

Figure 3.   Significant wave height during the passage of Hurricane Gustav, as measured by National Oceanic and Atmospheric Administration Buoy 42007.

2.4 Storm Surge

Measurements of maximum storm surge during Hurricane Gustav were made by coastal tide gages operated by NOAA (Beven and Kimberlain, 2009). As Gustav approached the Gulf Coast, water levels rose from the west coast of Florida to eastern Louisiana. Maximum storm surge ranged from 0.47 to 0.77 m along the west coast of Florida. Along the Florida panhandle and Alabama coasts, maximum storm surge was around 1 m. Closer to landfall, storm surge values of 3.01 m and 2.97 m were recorded at Bay-Waveland Yacht Club, Mississippi, 130 km east of landfall, and Shell Beach, Louisiana, 100 km east of landfall. At Grand Isle, the town closest to landfall, the storm surge reached only 1.37 m. West of landfall, from Amerada Pass to Sabine Pass, Louisiana, water levels decreased due to offshore winds as the storm approached. One to two days after landfall, maximum surge values of 0.4 to 1.1 m were recorded as the storm moved inland.

3. USGS Coastal-Change Observations

The USGS National Assessment of Coastal Change Hazards Project responded to Hurricane Gustav with the following data collection missions:
- Post-storm oblique aerial photography (completed September 4, 2008)
- Post-storm airborne lidar topographic survey (completed September 8, 2008)
- Ground-based control surveys (completed September 8, 2008)

The near-real-time responses of these efforts are documented at *http://coastal.er.usgs.gov/hurricanes/gustav/*.

Photographs taken of the barrier island coasts after the storm were matched to pre-storm images to locate areas of extreme erosion and accretion and damage to infrastructure. Post-storm photos were used to plan lidar mapping missions to target areas that were heavily affected by the storm and that experienced significant coastal change. The updated topography from this mission was compared to pre-storm topography to estimate changes in shoreline position, dune elevation, and infrastructure. The post-storm topography also serves as an update for emergency and coastal managers who require detailed knowledge of the post-storm landscape.

3.1 Oblique Aerial Photography and Video Observations

The USGS oblique digital photography (stills and video) is collected prior to hurricane landfall and immediately after landfall. Pre-storm photography is conducted immediately prior to landfall if logistically feasible; otherwise, baseline photography is used. Images are geo-located using Global Positioning System (GPS) positions that are recorded separately and merged with the imagery in post-processing. The compact digital video/digital photographic system (fig. 4) has been used on various aircraft such as the NOAA de Havilland Twin Otter, the Coast Guard H-60 and H-65 helicopters, and commercial Beechcraft King Air and Piper Navajo Chieftain aircraft.

Post-storm oblique aerial photography and video of the region of landfall were collected from a twin-engine King Air aircraft on September 4, 2008, 3 days after landfall. In total, 862 digital photographs and 5 hours of video were obtained over a 100-km extent from Grand Isle to Trinity Island, Louisiana, and over the Chandeleur Islands, which form the eastern flank of Louisiana. The photography sample rate was 0.5 frames/second (s) (or approximately 1 photo per 200 m along the coast). Examples of both pre- and post-storm photographs obtained during these two flights are shown in Section 4.1.

Figure 4.   Digital-photography and video recording system used aboard aircraft during coastal oblique video and photography missions.

3.2 Lidar Topographic Survey Techniques

High-resolution lidar systems can map hundreds of kilometers of coast in a day with point densities exceeding one point per square meter. High point densities combined with reasonable horizontal and vertical accuracies allow for the creation of topographic and bathymetric digital-elevation models (DEM) that show details of the coastal environment. Lidar systems emit pulses of light that reflect off the Earth's surface, allowing the computation of elevation from the two-way transmission time. The high-frequency pulses are emitted from a laser that is mounted on a small aircraft. Aircraft movement is monitored by an inertial navigation unit, a GPS unit, and tilt sensors. More complete descriptions of coastal lidar instruments and methods can be found in Brock and others (2002).

Lidar surveys receive positioning control using differential GPS, which requires a base-station receiver on the ground. The USGS sets up base stations near the area of hurricane impact if continuously operating reference stations (CORS) are not available. Additionally, because slowly varying positioning errors can corrupt the data (Sallenger and others, 2003), control points are surveyed for use in identifying these errors. Control points on surfaces that do not vary, such as roads or parking lots, can be obtained using ground-based surveying methods or by utilizing previous lidar surveys. Ground-based surveys performed on the beach surface are required to be synchronous with the lidar survey because of the likelihood for rapid and significant beach changes associated with the storm and the post-storm recovery period. Vertical accuracy of the lidar survey data is expected to be on the order of 10-20 centimeters (cm) (Sallenger and others, 2003), whereas the horizontal-position accuracy is on the order of 1 m (Nayegandhi and others, 2009).

After collection, the lidar data are processed using software written specifically for the lidar instrument. Included in the processing steps are removal of spurious data points and separation of points into first- and last-return lidar products (Bonisteel and others, 2009), which are selected from the first and last backscatter to return to the sensor from the laser pulse. First returns can be used to estimate canopy height in vegetated areas or rooftop height in developed areas, while last returns can be used to estimate elevation of the bare-Earth surface under vegetation.

3.2.1 Lidar Flight Information

An airborne lidar survey of post-storm topography was completed September 8, 2008, 7 days after landfall, on the barrier island coasts of Louisiana, Mississippi, Alabama, and Florida between Isles Dernieres, Louisiana, and Fort Walton Beach, Florida, using the USGS Experimental Advanced Airborne Research Lidar (EAARL) system. The EAARL system was mounted on a twin-engine Cessna 310 aircraft. The survey covered 570 km of coastline in 4 days. (See table 1 for details of each mission date.)

Table 1. September 4-8, 2008 post-Gustav EAARL lidar missions.

Date	Points (million)	Flight Time (hrs)	Number of Passes[1]	GPS Base Stations	Coverage Area
September 5, 2008	51	5.84	16	KHSA, Chandeleurs	Chandeleur Islands, Louisiana
September 6, 2008	52	6.20	4-6	KHSA, Chandeleurs, Grand Isle	Isles Dernieres to Southwest Pass, Louisiana
September 7, 2008	28	3.16	2-8	KHSA, Chandeleurs	Isles Dernieres to Grand Isle, Louisiana
September 8, 2008	29	3.33	2-5	KHSA, Dauphin Island	Ship Island, Mississippi to Fort Walton Beach, Florida

[1]Each pass overlaps the adjacent pass by 30-50 percent.

3.2.2 Lidar Control GPS Base-Stations

Ground-based survey systems were set up near Stennis International Airport, Mississippi (KHSA), on an island in the Chandeleur Islands, Louisiana, on Grand Isle, Louisiana, and on Dauphin Island, Alabama (fig. 5). New control points were created for each survey location. Instrumentation details and precise locations, including ellipsoidal height, for each station are listed in table 2.

Table 2. Details of the GPS control stations used during the September 5-8, 2008 EAARL lidar mission.

Station ID	North Latitude	West Longitude	Ellipsoidal Height (WGS84), in meters	Antenna Type
KHSA	30° 22' 25.83877"	89° 27' 09.39701"	-21.886	ASH 700936 A_M
Chandeleurs	29° 57' 12.70332"	88° 49' 38.42078"	-25.125	ASH 700936 A_M
Grand Isle	29° 15' 53.29737"	89° 57' 27.10763"	-22.942	ASH 700936 A_M
Dauphin Island	30° 14' 58.83936"	88° 04' 33.70120"	-24.589	ASH 700936 A_M

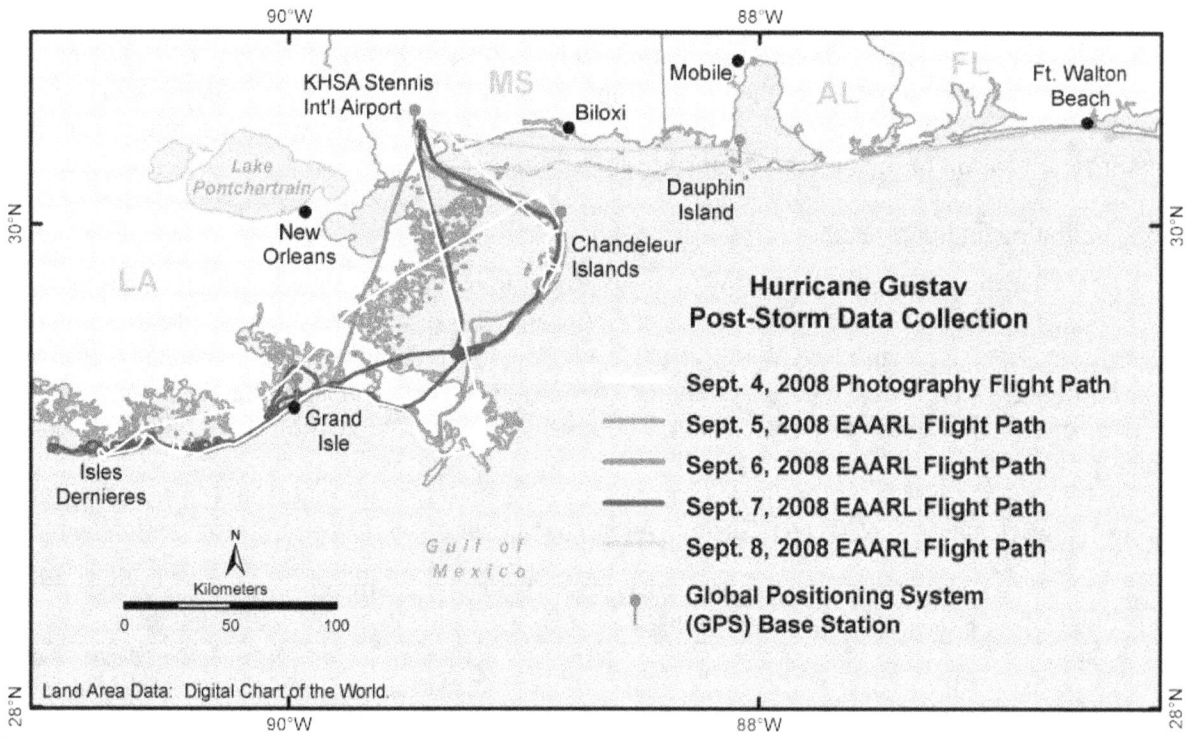

Figure 5. Hurricane Gustav post-storm oblique aerial photography and video flights, lidar coverage, and GPS base station locations.

3.2.3 Lidar Quality

Last-return lidar points were interpolated to a series of regular 5x5-m grid domains. The interpolation method applies a smoothing filter that removes short-scale variability and determines the degree to which residual noise has been removed (Plant and others, 2002). Elevations at grid points that received too few observations were removed to reduce system noise. Evaluation of the actual vertical accuracy of the lidar was performed against ground-based surveying (fig. 6). On Grand Isle, a ground survey was conducted by NOAA in October 2002 using a kinematic GPS mounted to a truck that was driven along Louisiana Route 1. The survey points were interpolated to a 5x5-m grid to match the lidar grid resolution. The offset between the gridded ground survey and the September 6-8, 2008, last-return gridded lidar data is -0.07 m (± 0.01), well within the expected vertical error of the lidar data (fig. 7). Because the ground survey was conducted in 2002 and the lidar survey in 2008, the 2 millimeter per year (mm/yr) subsidence at Grand Isle (Morton and Bernier, in press) may affect the comparison of the two surveys. However, the vertical accuracy of the lidar is within the range of the expected subsidence, so we cannot determine if the offset is due to lidar error or subsidence.

8

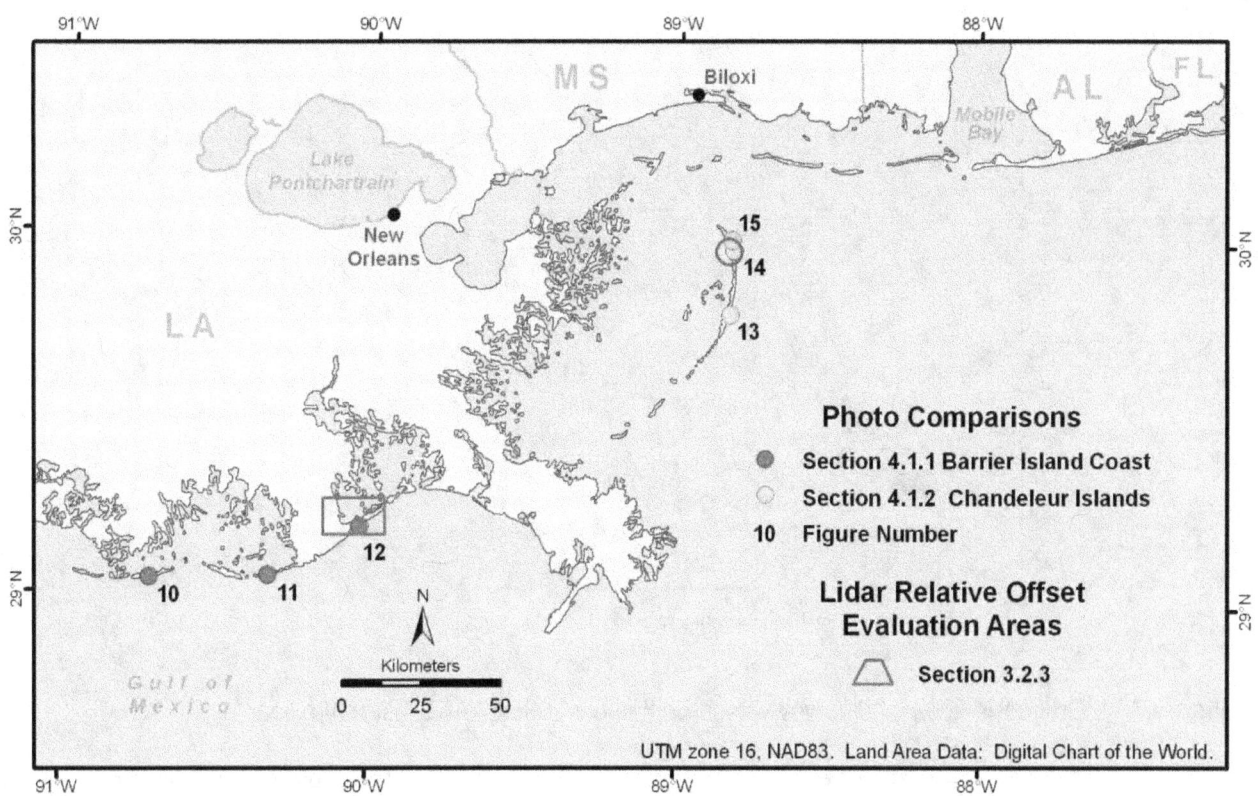

Figure 6. Map of lidar relative offset evaluation areas and location index for photo pairs (figs. 10-15). The red square shows location of the Grand Isle road survey. The red circle shows the location of the Chandeleur Islands ground survey. Photo pairs 10-12 from the central Louisiana barrier island coast are denoted as purple circles and photo pairs 13-15 from the Chandeleur Islands, Louisiana, are denoted as green circles.

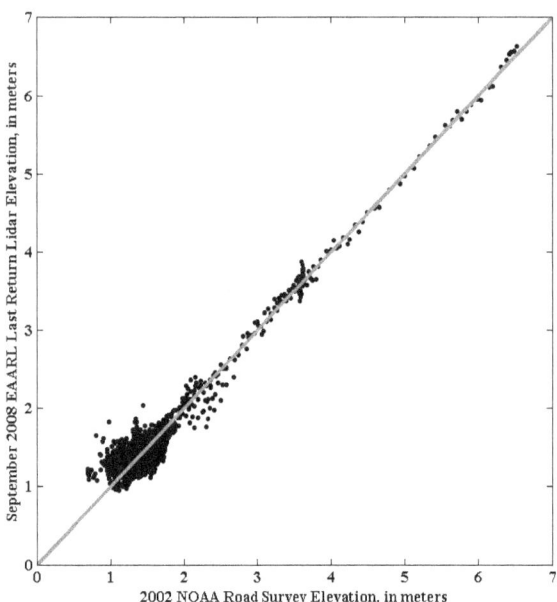

Figure 7. Grand Isle 2002 road survey versus September 2008 EAARL last-return lidar.

A USGS ground survey was conducted on the Chandeleur Islands, Louisiana, on September 5, 2008, simultaneous with the EAARL lidar flight. The survey used a kinematic GPS mounted on a buggy to survey 90,000 square meters (m^2) of the low-lying beach and marsh. The survey points were interpolated to a 5x5-m grid to match the lidar grid resolution. The offset between the gridded ground survey and the September 5, 2008, last-return gridded lidar data is +0.08 m ($\pm$ 0.08), well within the expected vertical error of the lidar data (fig. 8). The pre-storm lidar datasets were also evaluated for vertical accuracy using ground-based surveys. The March 9, 2008, and June 24-26, 2008, EAARL lidar surveys had no significant bias when compared to ground survey data. Since no ground surveys were conducted concurrent with the June 27-30, 2007, lidar survey, a relative offset between the 2007 and September 2008 data was determined. Lidar data were selected from a number of small areas containing fixed, flat features, such as roads, parking lots, and large buildings on Dauphin Island, Alabama. Grid cells were then selected based on their spatial error (normalized sampling error less than 25 percent and residual error less than 20 cm) to eliminate cells with a small number of observations or high noise due to system behavior, vegetation, or other sources of clutter. The selected grid cells were used to determine the relative offset of + 0.44 m ($\pm$ 0.22) (fig. 9), indicating that the 2007 survey was biased low compared to the 2008 survey. The 0.44 m bias has been corrected in the 2007 dataset, since the September 2008 dataset agrees with the ground-control points collected concurrently with the lidar survey.

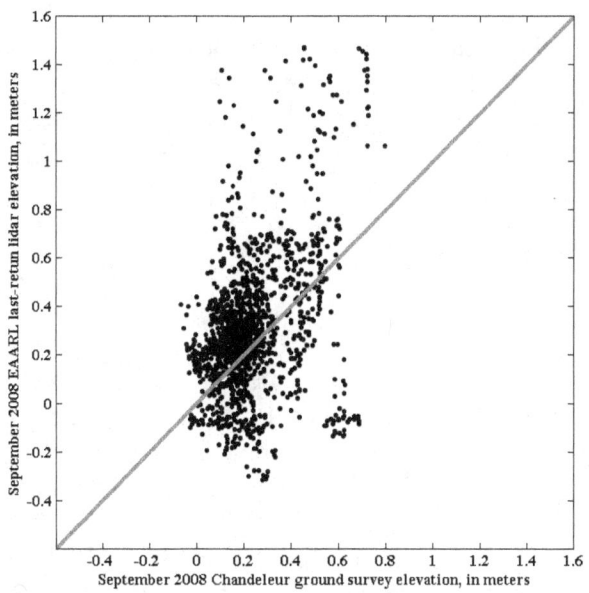

Figure 8. September 2008 Chandeleur Island ground survey versus 2008 EAARL last-return lidar.

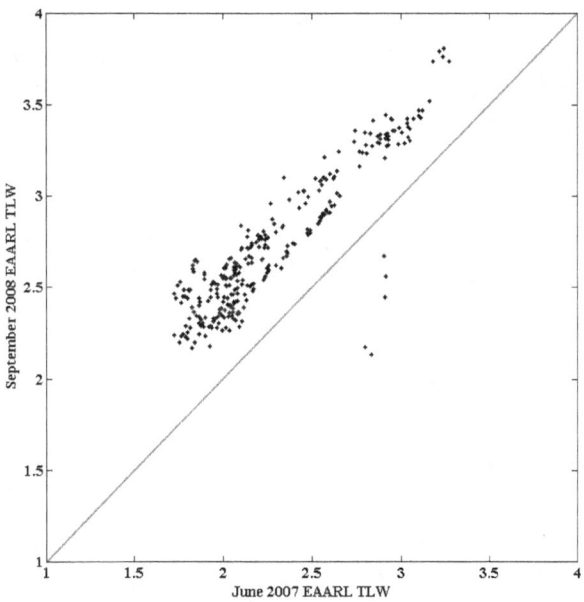

Figure 9. Relative offset between June 2007 and September 2008 EAARL last-return lidar on Dauphin Island.

4. Coastal-Change Analysis

Comparisons of pre- and post-storm photography were used to identify examples of coastal changes that span the range of responses to the hurricane conditions. Pre- and post-storm lidar topographic surveys were compared to quantify the spatial extent and magnitude of these coastal changes. The quantitative analyses include estimates of changes in dune height, shoreline position, and sediment volume.

4.1 Photo Comparison Analysis

4.1.1 Barrier Island Coast of Central Louisiana

The barrier island coast of central Louisiana has been subjected, in places, to relatively rapid rates of historic shoreline erosion. For example, between 1887 and 1996, the shoreline shown in the photos from East Timbalier Island (see fig. 11) retreated landward about 20 m/yr (Penland and others, 2003). The central coast of Louisiana has also been subjected to repeated and severe hurricanes. For example, three hurricanes, Lili (October 3, 2002), Katrina (August 29, 2005) and Rita (September 24, 2005), made landfall along this stretch of coast in the 6 years before Gustav (figs. 10-12). During Gustav, the Louisiana barrier island coast experienced additional loss of sand from the already narrow beaches (fig. 10). East Timbalier Island (fig. 11) experienced significant beach and marsh losses during Hurricane Rita which fragmented the island. Hurricane Gustav further degraded the island by eroding sand and narrowing the beach.

The community of Grand Isle, Louisiana (fig. 12), was likely overwashed and inundated during Hurricane Gustav as high surge and waves overtopped the island. Evidence of inundation includes scouring due to flows across the island. Grand Isle does not appear to have been inundated during Hurricane Rita and was likely protected from inundation by the initially wider beach and extensive dune vegetation at that time. Extensive erosion during Rita left a lower, narrower beach that likely allowed further damage during Gustav.

29° 2.75' N 90° 43.09' W

Figure 10. Oblique aerial photography of Trinity Island, Isles Dernieres, Louisiana, from July 18, 2001 (top); September 30, 2005, 6 days after the landfall of Hurricane Rita (middle); and September 4, 2008, 3 days after the landfall of Hurricane Gustav (bottom). Yellow cross-hairs indicate a common reference location within the images. Shoreline erosion is the main coastal-change impact seen in this location.

Figure 11. Oblique aerial photography of East Timbalier, Louisiana, from July 18, 2001 (top); September 30, 2005, 6 days after the landfall of Hurricane Rita (middle); and September 4, 2008, 3 days after the landfall of Hurricane Gustav (bottom). Yellow cross-hairs indicate a common reference location within the images. Hurricane Gustav further degraded this area by eroding sand and narrowing the beach.

Figure 12. Oblique aerial photography of Grand Isle, Louisiana, from July 18, 2001 (top); September 30, 2005, 6 days after the landfall of Hurricane Rita (middle); and September 4, 2008, 3 days after the landfall of Hurricane Gustav (bottom). Coastal-change impacts include beach and dune erosion, removal of dune vegetation, and inundation. Evidence of inundation includes scouring due to flows across the island, seen in the standing water and sand deposits located seaward of the large white building and road.

4.1.2 Chandeleur Islands, Louisiana

The Chandeleur Islands form the eastern flank of Louisiana and have historically eroded landward at an average of about 9 m/yr (Penland and others, 2003). Past hurricanes, such as Camille in 1969, have breached the islands in many places. After each storm, the islands have recovered, at least to some extent, and many of the breaches have closed. During Hurricane Katrina (August 29, 2005), however, the island lost 85 percent of its surface area in a few hours and has struggled afterwards to rebuild naturally. In the 3 years since the storm, over 50 percent of the shore has continued to erode, though some recovery is evident (figs. 13-14). Hurricane Gustav (September 1, 2008) appears to have set back any recovery of the islands even further, by waves overwashing sand landward and attacking the marsh platforms on which the beach and dunes of the Chandeleurs are built (figs. 13-15).

Figure 13.   Oblique aerial photography of the central Chandeleur Islands, Louisiana, from July 17, 2001 (top left); August 31, 2005, 2 days after the landfall of Hurricane Katrina (top right); June 24, 2008 (bottom left); and September 4, 2008, 3 days after the landfall of Hurricane Gustav (bottom right). Yellow cross-hairs indicate a common reference location within the images. Sand was eroded from the beach face and transported landward by waves.

Figure 14. Oblique aerial photography of the northern Chandeleur Islands, Louisiana, from July 17, 2001 (top left); August 31, 2005, 2 days after the landfall of Hurricane Katrina (top right); June 24, 2008 (bottom left); and September 4, 2008, 3 days after the landfall of Hurricane Gustav (bottom right). Yellow cross-hairs indicate a common reference location within the images. Sand was eroded from the beach face and transported landward by waves, resulting in an increasingly smaller and more fragmented island.

Figure 15. Oblique aerial photography of the northern tip of the Chandeleur Islands, Louisiana, from July 17, 2001 (top left); August 31, 2005, 2 days after the landfall of Hurricane Katrina (top right); June 24, 2008 (bottom left); and September 4, 2008, 3 days after the landfall of Hurricane Gustav (bottom right). Yellow cross-hairs indicate a common reference location within the images. The sand that had deposited since Hurricane Katrina was removed from the island, leaving only a small marsh platform.

4.2 Quantitative Topographic-Change Analysis

Post-storm lidar topographic data were compared to pre-storm surveys of beach topography to quantify morphologic changes due to Hurricane Gustav. Because of the large spatial extent of the post-storm lidar survey, several different survey dates had to be used for the pre-storm topography. The survey date and spatial coverage for each pre-storm survey are detailed in table 3. For morphologic analysis, last-return lidar data were optimized for identifying shorelines and dune height. The analysis required interpolation to a gridded domain that was rotated parallel to the shoreline and had a resolution of 10 m in the longshore direction and 2.5 m in the cross-shore direction. The interpolation method applies spatial filtering with a Hanning window that is twice as wide as the grid resolution (Plant and others, 2002). Grids of pre- and post-storm lidar topography differenced over the entire overlapping survey area provide a quick visual of coastal change. For example, in Dauphin Island, Alabama, difference grids reveal erosion of the shoreline and reduction of dune elevations (fig. 16). The emergency berm built after Hurricane Katrina (fig. 16) has been completely eroded by the waves and surge generated by Hurricane Gustav.

For a more quantitative analysis, gridded last-return lidar data were used to measure changes in elevation and position of the frontal sand dune or berm system, shoreline change, and volume change. The cross-shore location of the peak elevation of the seaward-most sand dune is extracted from gridded pre-storm topography (Stockdon and others, in press). The difference between the pre- and post-storm topography at this location defines hurricane-induced dune or berm-elevation change (figs. 17A-20A).

To calculate the shoreline position, the cross-shore position of the elevation at the shoreline (defined in regard to a vertical datum) was extracted from each row of the shore-parallel-oriented grids of beach topography (Stockdon and others, 2002). The shoreline vertical datum was set at mean high water from tidal records (Weber and others, 2005) and is approximately 0.37 m above mean sea level for Isles Dernieres to Venice, Louisiana, and approximately 0.23 m above mean sea level from the Chandeleur Islands, Louisiana to Fort Walton Beach, Florida. Shoreline change was calculated as the difference between the pre-storm shoreline and the post-storm horizontal shoreline position (figs. 17B-20B). Typical errors in shoreline position are on the order of 1 to 2 m (Stockdon and others, 2002); however uncertainty in position will vary due to data noise and beach slope.

Volume-change calculations were performed by contouring the topography at a fixed vertical datum, which was set at mean high water from tidal records (Weber and others, 2005). The volume is calculated between the cross-shore location of the pre-storm dune base and the pre-storm shoreline. This eliminates complications from structures and vegetation, which generally are located landward of the dune base. Beach volume change was calculated as the difference between the pre-storm and September 2008 surveys (figs. 17C-20C).

Table 3. Details of the pre-storm lidar data used for coastal-change analysis.

Survey Date	Instrument	Spatial Coverage
June 27-29, 2007	EAARL	Ship Island, Mississippi, to Petit Bois Island, Mississippi
March 9, 2008	EAARL	Isles Dernieres, Louisiana, to Venice, Louisiana
June 24-26, 2008	EAARL	Dauphin Island, Alabama, to Ft. Walton Beach, Florida, and Chandeleur Islands, Louisiana

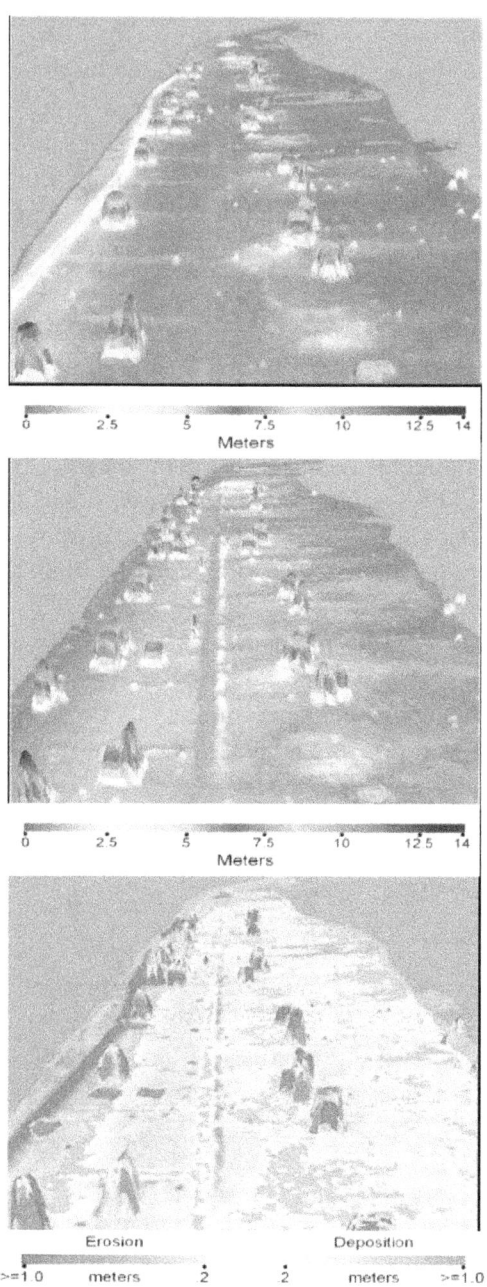

Figure 16. Three-dimensional view of Dauphin Island, Alabama, lidar-based topography measured in June 2007 (top) and September 8, 2008 (middle). Blue represents elevations below mean high water. Lower elevations are represented by brown shades; higher elevations are greens and reds. The view is looking west along the island with the Gulf of Mexico to left. A 3.5-m emergency berm that was built after Hurricane Katrina (2005), seen in green on the Gulf-side of the island in 2007 (top), is conspicuously absent post-Gustav (middle). The bottom image shows changes in elevation with areas of erosion in red and deposition in green. Sand eroded from the beach was deposited inland. Overwash along the road was cleared prior to the lidar flight. Piles of cleared sand are seen in green along the north side of the road. The patches of red and green on the houses are an artifact of data processing. Large green rectangles on the ground are locations of houses built since Hurricane Katrina.

4.2.1 Barrier Island Coast of Central Louisiana

Dune-height changes ranging from 1 to 2 m were observed in the Isles Dernieres, where Gustav made landfall. Similar dune-height changes were observed at Grand Isle, Louisiana, about 60 km from landfall and in the right-front quadrant of the storm impact area (fig. 17A). Mean shoreline erosion of 40 m was observed on the central Louisiana coast from Trinity Island to Grand Isle, Louisiana (fig. 17B). On the eastern and western ends of Timbalier Island, more extreme shoreline erosion of 100 to 200 m was observed. Volume losses follow the same pattern as the shoreline changes for the central Louisiana barrier islands (fig. 17C), implying that sediment lost due to erosion was transported seaward and not deposited higher on the beach face.

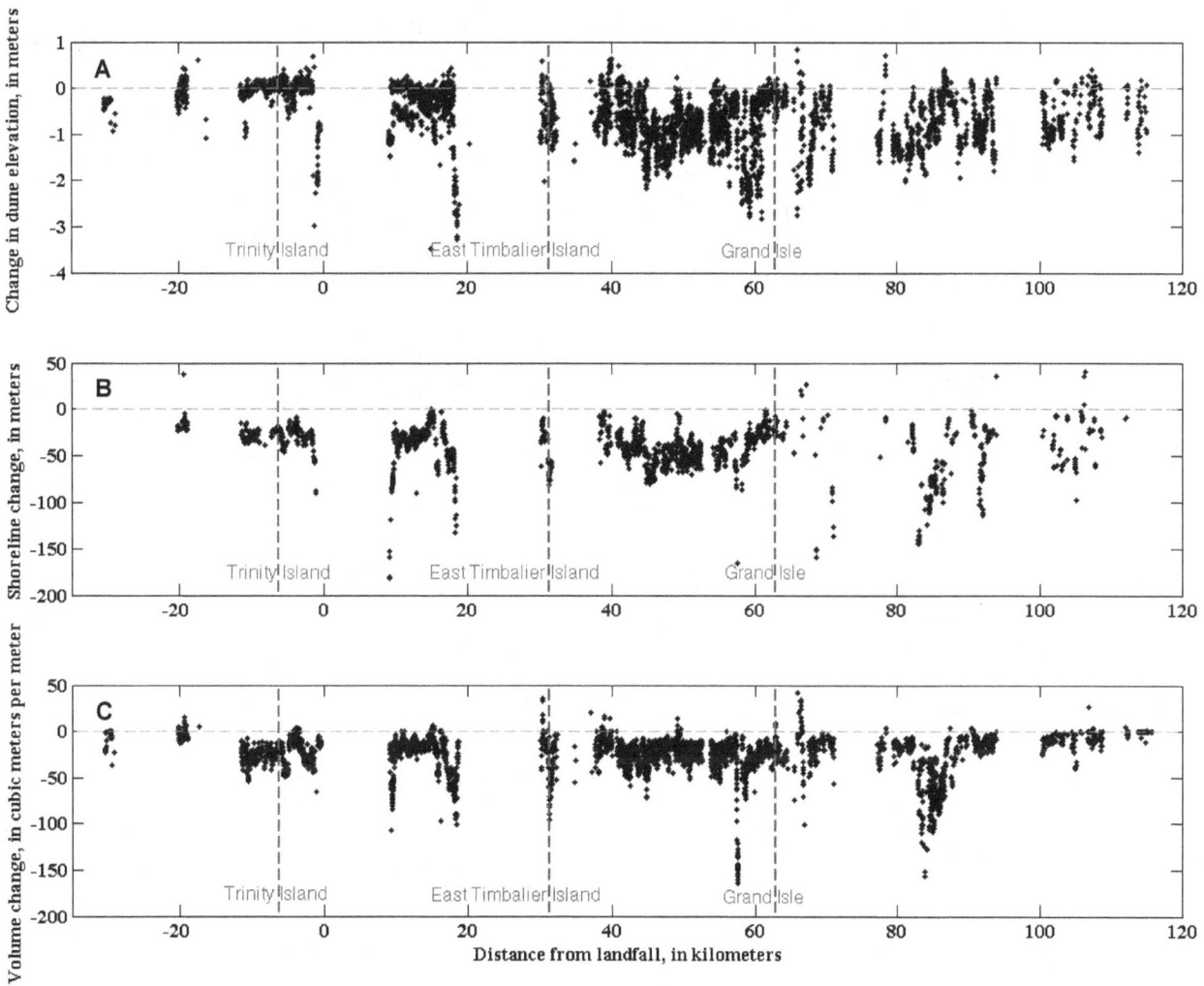

Figure 17. Hurricane Gustav dune-elevation change (A), shoreline change (B), and beach-volume change (C) between March and September 2008 for the central Louisiana barrier island coast. Vertical dashed lines indicate the center of Trinity Island (the easternmost of the three islands composing the Isles Dernieres), East Timbalier Island, and the town of Grand Isle, Louisiana.

4.2.2 Mississippi Barrier Island Coast

Along the Mississippi barrier island coast, 150 to 200 km to the east of landfall, mean dune-height changes were near zero (fig. 18A), with the exception of the ~1-m elevation change on the western end of Horn Island. Shoreline change was highly variable ranging from extreme erosion of 100 to 200 m on East Ship Island to accretion of ~100 m near the center of Horn Island , where there is an inflection point in the shoreline orientation (fig. 18B). Because the pre-storm survey is from June 2007, the shoreline changes seen here may be a combination of long-term and storm-induced change. Similar to the Louisiana sandy barriers, volume losses here follow the same pattern as shoreline changes (fig. 18C).

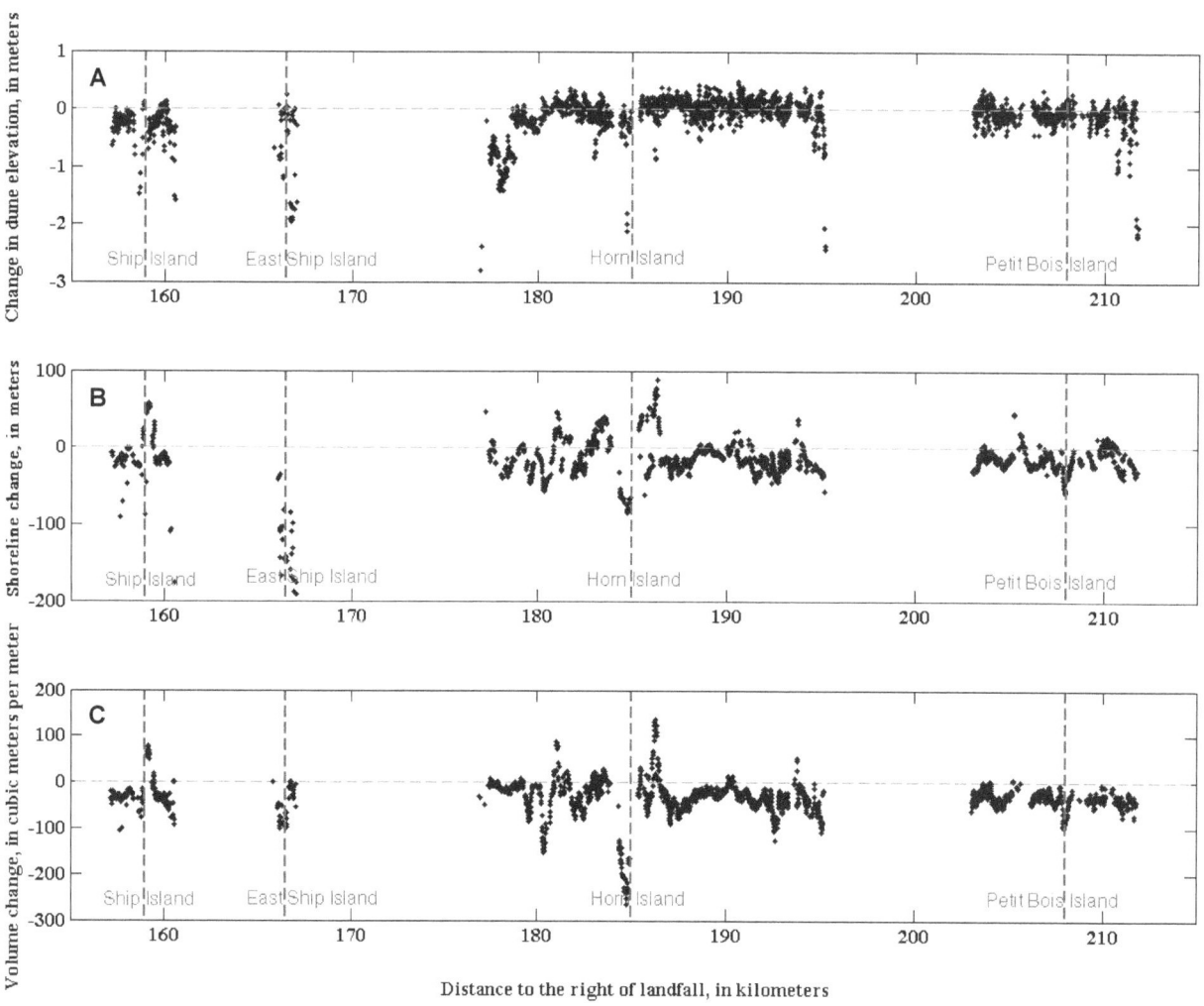

Figure 18. Hurricane Gustav dune-elevation change (*A*), shoreline change (*B*), and beach-volume change (*C*) between June 2007 and September 2008 for the Mississippi barrier island coast. Vertical dashed lines indicate the center of West Ship Island, East Ship Island, Horn Island, and Petit Bois Island.

4.2.3 Alabama Barrier Island Coast

On Dauphin Island, Alabama, 230 km to the east of landfall, mean dune-height changes were also near zero except for the 3-m elevation loss resulting from the destruction of the post-Katrina emergency berm, located between 230 and 240 km from landfall (fig. 19A). The native dunes on Dauphin Island are wider and more vegetated than the manmade emergency berm and resisted the severe erosion that impacted the manmade berm. Mean dune-height changes were near zero for the Alabama barrier island coast east of Dauphin Island (fig. 19A). Average shoreline erosion of 20 m was observed from Dauphin Island, Alabama, to Orange Beach, Alabama, with the exception of the areas of accretion on the spits of Dauphin Island (fig. 19B). Volume losses mirror the same pattern as the shoreline changes for the Alabama barrier island coast (fig. 19C).

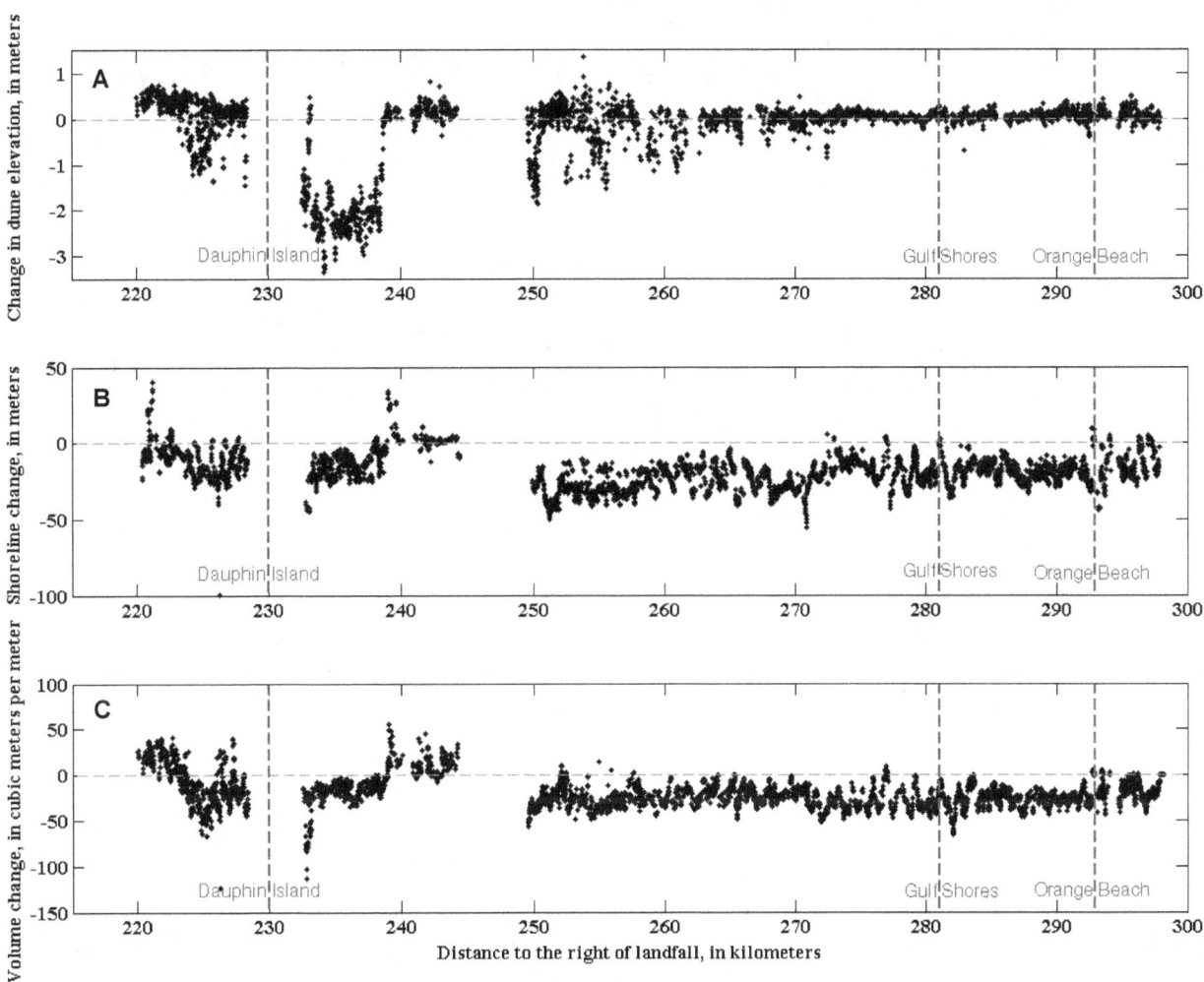

Figure 19. Hurricane Gustav dune-elevation change (*A*), shoreline change (*B*), and beach-volume change (*C*) between June and September 2008 for the Alabama barrier island coast. Vertical dashed lines indicate the center of Dauphin Island, and the towns of Gulf Shores and Orange Beach, Alabama.

4.2.4 Florida Barrier Island Coast

Dune-height changes were near zero for the barrier island coast of the Florida Panhandle (fig. 20A). Shoreline erosion ranged from 20 m on Perdido Key, Florida, to 0 m east of Gulf Breeze, Florida (fig. 20B). From the western end of Santa Rosa Island (fig. 20B, distance = 320 km), to Gulf Breeze, Florida, shoreline erosion of 50 to 60 m was observed. Volume losses were small but indicate that some sand was eroded even though the shoreline position and dune height changes were near zero (fig. 20C).

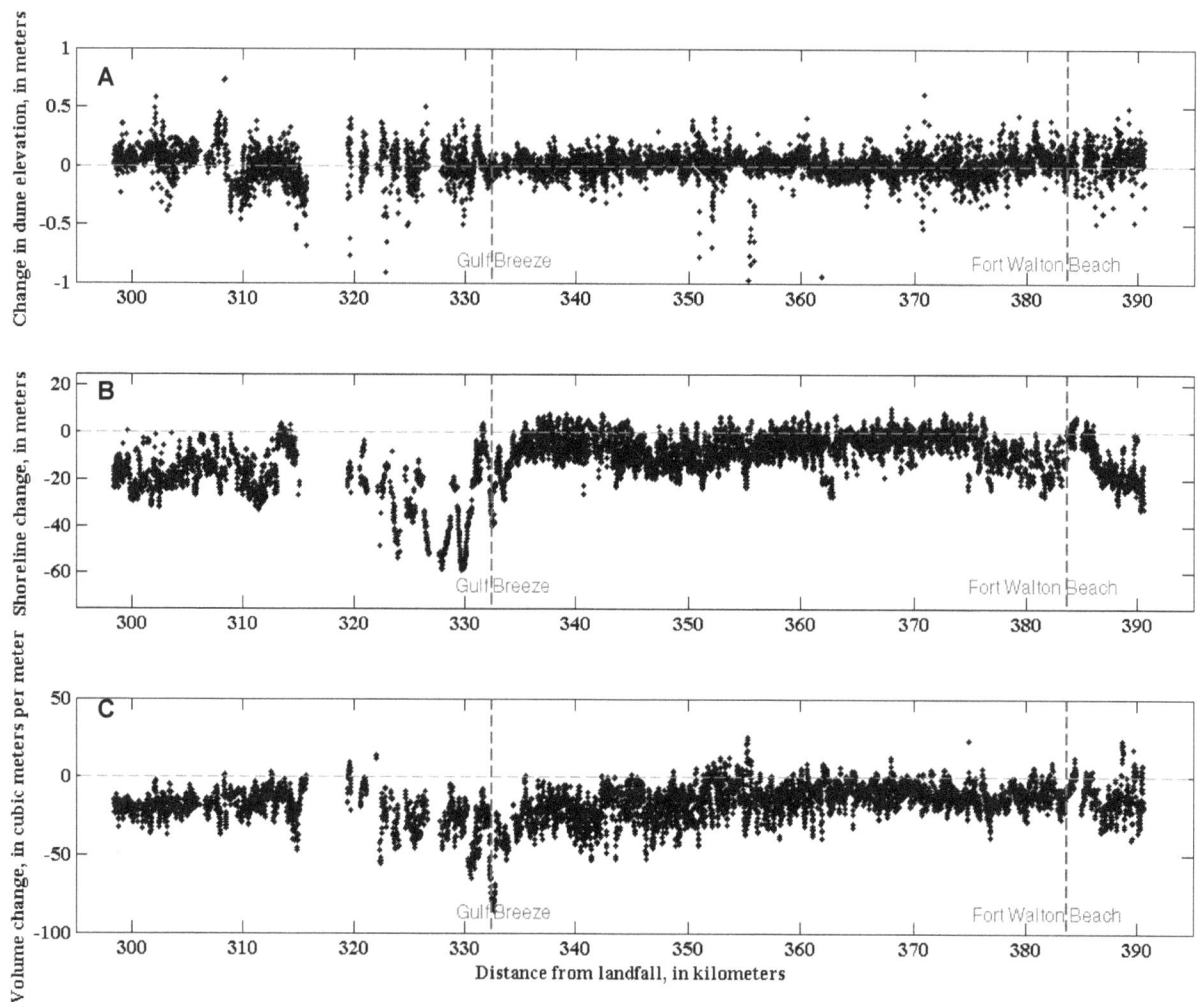

Figure 20. Hurricane Gustav dune-elevation change (*A*), shoreline change (*B*), and beach-volume change (*C*) between June and September 2008 for the Florida panhandle barrier island coast. Vertical dashed lines indicate the center of the towns of Gulf Breeze and Fort Walton Beach, Florida.

4.2.5 Chandeleur Islands, Louisiana

Because the Chandeleur Islands are low-lying marsh platforms fronted by transient sandy beaches, different methodologies were used to quantify storm-induced topographic change. Instead of measuring dune-elevation change, the maximum elevation was computed within a 5-m-wide swath oriented south to north and covering the width of the island (fig. 21). The maximum elevation change observed between June and September 2008 was on the order of 0.5 m to 1 m of erosion. Island area above the mean high water line is computed in ArcGIS using contours at 0.23 m. Between June and September 2008 the islands lost 23 percent of the existing land area (fig. 22). The islands have migrated westward and become increasingly fragmented as a result of the large waves and surge of Hurricane Gustav.

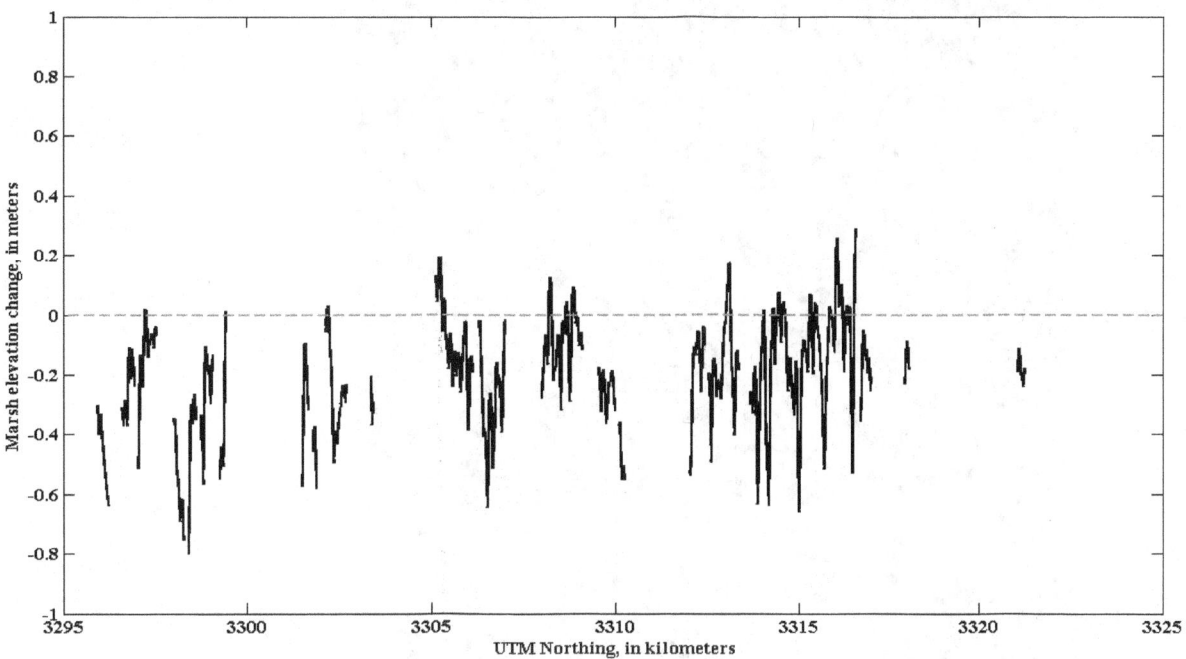

Figure 21. Chandeleur Islands change in maximum elevation between June and September 2008.

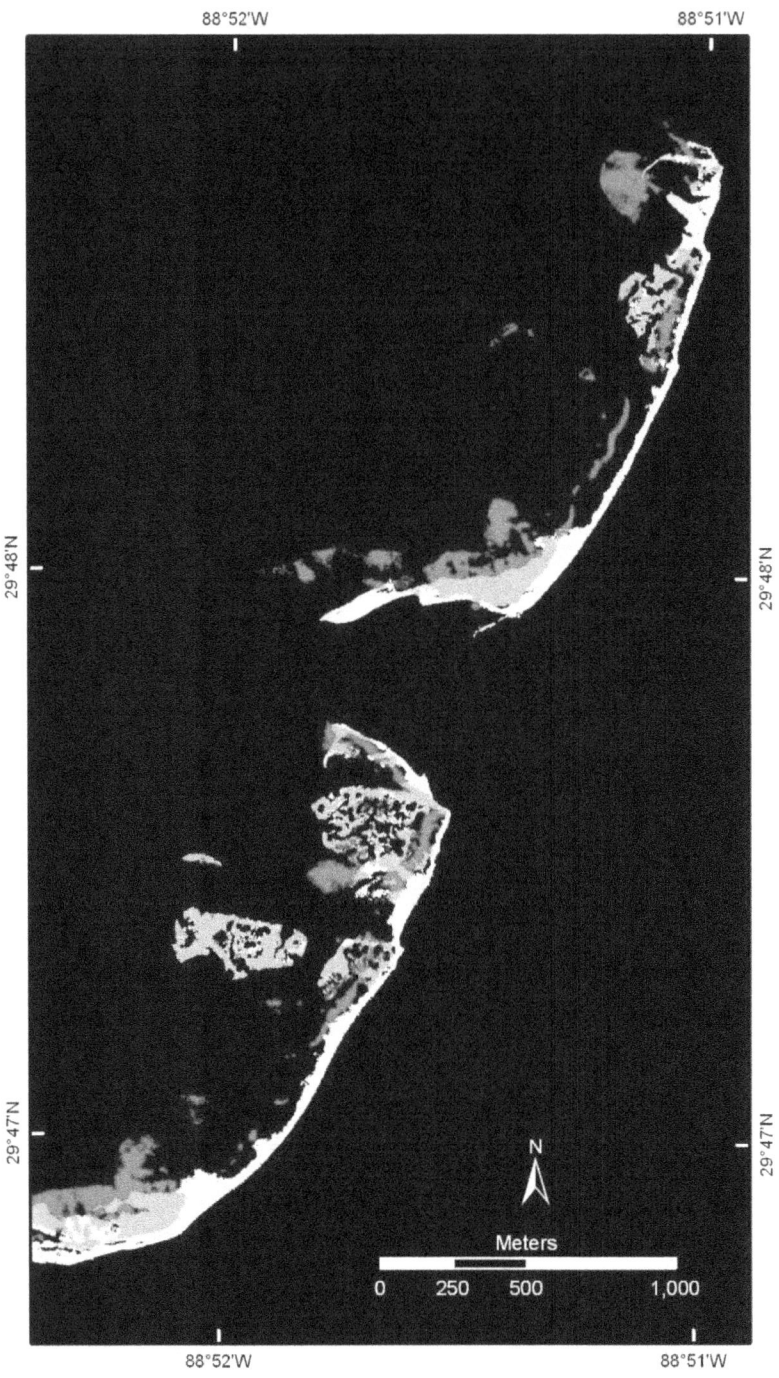

Figure 22. Chandeleur Islands area in June (yellow) and September 2008 (red) for the 4-km portion of the coast shown in figures 13 and 14. The orange color indicates area common to both dates, revealing patterns of erosion and deposition. The yellow areas were eroded and deposited landward in the red areas. These patterns are representative of area change observations for the entire Chandeleur Island chain.

5. Acknowledgments

The USGS National Assessment of Coastal Change Hazards Project thanks the many scientists and support staff who invested long hours during the 2008 hurricane season. Specifically, we thank the EAARL research team (Wayne Wright and Richard Mitchell) and ground surveyors (B.J. Reynolds and Nancy DeWitt). Colleagues in the St. Petersburg office helped with data collection (Dennis Krohn, Karen Morgan), processing and analysis (Charlene Sullivan, Peter Howd, Mark Hansen, Dave Thompson, and Ann Marie Ascough), and web page development (Jolene Shirley).

6. References Cited

Beven, J.L. II, and Kimberlain, T.B., 2009, Tropical cyclone report Hurricane Gustav: National Oceanic and Atmospheric Administration National Hurricane Center Report AL072008, 36 p.

Bonisteel, J.M., Nayegandhi, Amar., Wright, C.W., Brock, J.C., and Nagle, D.B., 2009, Experimental Advanced Airborne Research Lidar (EAARL) data processing manual: U.S. Geological Survey Open-File Report 2009-1078, 38 p.

Brock, J.C., Wright, C.W., Sallenger, A.H., Krabill, W.B.., and Swift, R.N., 2002, Basis and methods of NASA airborne topographic mapper lidar surveys for coastal studies: Journal of Coastal Research, v. 18, no. 1, p. 1-13.

Morton, R.A. and Bernier, J.C., in press, Recent subsidence-rate reductions in the Mississippi delta and their geological implications: Journal of Coastal Research.

National Data Buoy Center, 2008, Reports from the National Data Buoy Center's stations during the passage of Hurricane Gustav: National Oceanic and Atmospheric Administration, accessed at *http://www.ndbc.noaa.gov/hurricanes/2008/gustav* on June 4, 2009.

Nayegandhi, Amar., Brock, J.C., and Wright, C.W., 2009, Small-footprint, waveform-resolving lidar estimation of submerged and sub-canopy topography in coastal environments: International Journal of Remote Sensing, v. 30, no. 4, p. 861-878.

Penland, Shea., Zganjar, Chris, Westphal, K.A, Connor, Paul, Beall, Andrew, List, Jeff and Williams, S.J., 2003, Shoreline change posters of the Louisiana Barrier Islands: 1885 to 1996: U.S. Geological Survey Open-File Report 2003-398, 8 sheets.

Plant, N.G., Holland, K.T. and Puleo, J.A., 2002, Analysis of the scale of errors in nearshore bathymetric data: Marine Geology, v. 191, no. 1-2, p. 71-86.

Powell, M.D., Houston, S.H., Amat, L.R., and Morisseau-Leroy, N., 1998, The HRD real-time hurricane wind analysis system: Journal of Wind Engineering and Industrial Aerodynamics, v. 77-78, p. 53-64.

Sallenger, A.H., Krabill, W.B., Swift, R.N., Brock, J., List, J., Hansen, Mark, Holman, R.A., Manizade, S., Sontag, J., Meredith, A., Morgan, K., Yunkel, J.K., Frederick, E.B., and Stockdon, H.F., 2003, Evaluation of airborne topographic lidar for quantifying beach changes: Journal of Coastal Research, v. 19 , no. 1, p. 125-133.

Stockdon, H., Sallenger, A., List, J., and Holman, R., 2002, Estimation of shoreline position and change using airborne topographic lidar data: Journal of Coastal Research, vol. 18, no. 3, p. 502-513.

Stockdon, H.F., Doran, K.S., and Sallenger, A.H., in press, Extraction of lidar-based dune-crest elevations for use in examining the vulnerability of beaches to inundation during hurricanes: Journal of Coastal Research Special Issue.

Weber, K.M., List, J.H., and Morgan, K.L.M., 2005, An operational mean high water datum for determination of shoreline position from topographic lidar data: U.S. Geological Survey Open-File Report 2005-1027, available online at *http://pubs.usgs.gov/of/2005/1027*.

www.ingramcontent.com/pod-product-compliance
Lightning Source LLC
Chambersburg PA
CBHW080351290526
45791CB00009BA/2830